SILV*

Myrrh, aloes, pollen and other traces

Botanical research on the Shroud

Translated by Alan Neame

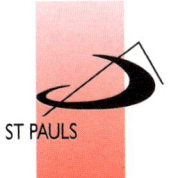

ST PAULS

Series: THE SHROUD OF TURIN

1. Shroud, Gospels and Christian life.
2. The Shroud under the microscope. Forensic examination.
3. On the trail of the Shroud. Early and recent history.
4. An 'inexplicable' image. Theories on how the image on the Shroud was formed.
5. The image on the Shroud. Results of photography and information technology.
6. Shroud, carbon dating and calculus of probabilities.
7. Myrrh, aloes, pollen and other traces. Botanical research on the Shroud.

On the front cover: Pollen grain of walnut (*Juglans regia* L.), enlarged 500 times by scanning electron microscope, showing the rounded form of the grain, the surface of its outer wall covered with small regular bumps, and the small pores piercing the extine. (Photo by R. Caramiello taken with ETEC Microscope at the Electronic Microscopy Centre of the University of Turin).

ST PAULS
Ireland
London SW1P 1EP, United Kingdom

© ST PAULS (UK) 1998

ISBN 085439 538 5

Set by TuKan, High Wycombe
Produced in the EC
Printed by The Guernsey Press Co. Ltd, Guernsey, C.I.

ST PAULS is an activity of the priests and brothers of the Society of St Paul who proclaim the Gospel through the media of social communication

CONTENTS

Bibliography 4

Why do botanical research on
   the Shroud? 5

Flax, the plant the Shroud is made of 12

From the flax plant to the Shroud fabric
   and its chemical composition 19

Plants that have left traces on the Shroud 26

Pollen and the history of the Shroud 44

Has the Shroud any botanical surprises
   in store? 57

BIBLIOGRAPHY

BAIMA BOLLONE P.L., *Sindone o no*.SEI Turin 1990.

BAR YOSEF O., *A cave in the desert: Nahal Nemar*. Cat. No. 258, The Israel Museum, Jerusalem 1985.

DONADONI ROVERI A.M., *Arte della tessitura, moda, arredo.* 218-231. In MUSEO EGIZIO (a cura di), *Civiltà degli Egizi: Vita quotidiana*. Isstituto Bancario San Paolo, Turin 1987.

FUJI H., *Al-Tar 1. Excavations in Iraq 1971-1976.* Tokyo 1976.

GEROLA F.M., (a cura di), Enciclopedia Motta. 'Il Mondo della natura', Botanica vol. 1. Federico Motta Editore, Milan 1962.

KIRTIKAR K.R., BASU B.D. AND AN I.C.S., *Inddian medicinal plants,* 3 vols. and 4 vols of Iconografy. International Book Distributors Booksellers. Dehra Dun. India 1935.

PIGNATTI, A., *Flora d'Italia*, 3 vols. Edagricole. Bologna 1982.

SAVIO P., *Ricerche sul tessuto della Santa Sindone*. Grottaferrata 1973.

SCANNERINI S., *La questione dei pollini. Sindon 1996*. Congresso Internazionale sulla Sindon 16-17 February 1996. San Marino 1996.

ZOHARY D., *The origin and early spread of agriculture in the old world.* In *The origin and domestication of cultivated plants*. Barigozzi, C. (ed), pp. 8-20. Elsevier. Amsterdam 1986.

ZOHARY M., *Flora palaestina.* 4 parts (8 vols). Israel Academy of Sciences and Humanities. Jerusalem 1966-1986.

ZOHARY M., *La flora della Bibbia*, in *Enciclopedia della Bibbia*, LDC Turin 1970.

Why do botanical research on the Shroud?

The Shroud and multi-disiplinary research

Today's scientific knowledge about the Shroud is the accumulated result of almost a century of laboratory work, of documentation, and of writings of varying scientific weight and usefulness, devoted to finding out what exactly the Shroud is. Taken together, all this constitutes an autonomous science: Sindonology. To crack the mystery, international research groups have debated and are debating topics that range from biology to physics, from forensic medicine to archaeology, from biblical exegesis to textile analysis. A review called *Sindon*, exclusively concerned with the data being acquired and with discussions on the Shroud, is published regularly in Turin. It accepts contributions of whatever provenance and publishes the acts of congresses specifically concerned with the Shroud.

I am aware, this being the case, that to devote an introductory booklet to the plants of the Shroud may sound like the hyper-specialised and pedantic self-indulgence of some botanist doomed to lose himself in a sea of research work which has nothing to do with botany at all. The theme of the winding-sheet attributed by religious and popular tradition to Jesus, the journey the sheet has apparently made, the carbon-dating episode: all this has been re-examined with a wealth of documentation and critical acumen in 1990 by a forensic scientist and sindonologist Pierluigi Bollone. What then is the point of a botanical booklet? . . .

So many tesserae, only one mosaic

With no lack of respect for something which, even for those who maintain its origin to be medieval, is nonetheless a remarkable icon of the passion of Jesus Christ – nor have we managed to discover how it was formed – the problem we have to solve, if we are to understand exactly what the Shroud is, lies in the sphere of forensic medicine. A detective story the solution to which, if it is ever found, will be a mosaic of *tesserae*, assembled one by one, over two thousand years

– from Christ's death to our own day – and five thousand kilometres from Palestine to Turin.

Thus all of us, from greatest to least, are aware of the Shroud's importance and attraction as a religious, historical and archaeological document, and are fascinated by the mysterious but indisputable traces of the Man of the Shroud, documenting his appearance and the story of a death by crucifixion impressively corresponding with the Gospel account of the death of Jesus Christ.

The world of plants (and more generally of all vegetation including micro-organisms, i.e. all botany) seems light-years away from the Shroud and I realise that opening an opuscule about the Shroud and Botany will have cost the future reader a certain effort.

Close links between the Shroud and Botany

And yet Shroud and Botany have scientific links just as close as those between Shroud and pathological anatomy, between Shroud and history, and between Shroud and archaeology. There is no doubt the amount of research still to be covered, far from being exhausted, has scarcely begun. If this is so, this little volume is not a display of pedantry but a modest and (let us hope) not too tedious attempt to introduce the reader to a method of study and a field of inquiry combining beauty with usefulness for a scientific understanding of the Shroud.

Indeed, the Shroud itself is a 'botanical' object, in as much as it is a cloth made of flax. Other vegetable matter (pollen, remains of oils and spices) makes up a considerable part of the traces on which we rely in reconstructing its history. Oils and spices extracted from ancient medicinal plants, and their vapours could have been partly responsible for the mysterious forming of the image. Masses of micro-organisms now present on the cloth could one day destroy it. Indeed, the recent and much discussed carbon-14 dating, which has 'rejuvenated' the Shroud by interpreting it as a medieval cloth, has been nothing other than the measuring of a physical characteristic of linen which, as a product made from a living organism capable of absorbing and fixing the carbon dioxide in the atmosphere, can act like a clock. Not only this: how much the Shroud's botanical features conceal and reveal about the landscape, about life in its centuries of existence, about the age in which it was woven, about burial customs, about the countries through which it has passed, and what indispensable clues these provide for anyone approaching the Turin relic in forensic terms, is probably not known to many people, but precisely for this reason deserves attention.

The purpose of this little book is indeed to usher the reader into the botanical world of the Shroud: where plants hold sway, such as flax, aloe, *Commiphora* (or myrrh) and thorns, as well

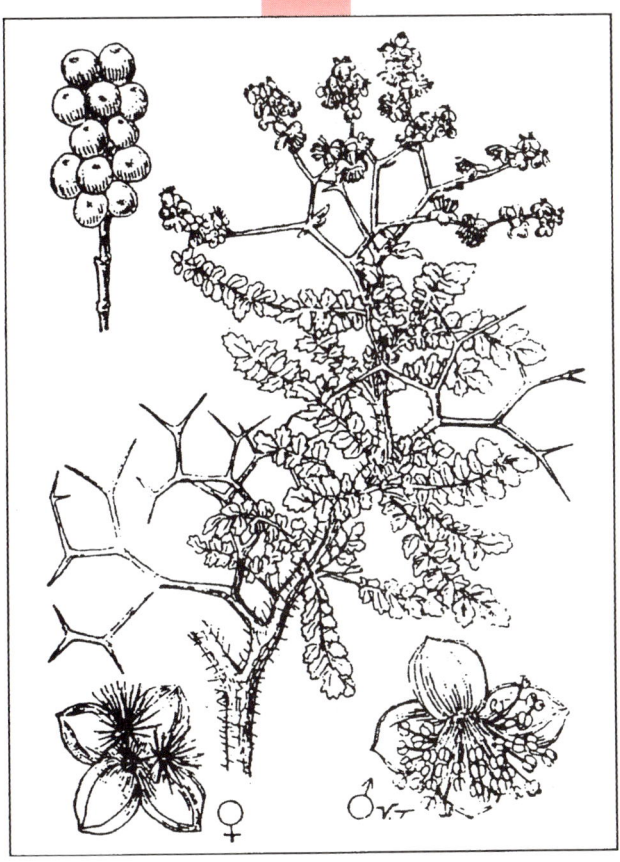

Fig. 1 – A plant and possible candidate for the crown of thorns: Sarcopoterium spinosum Schrantz (= Poterium spinosum L.), *the crown of thorns, replacing the more famous* Paliurus spina-Christi Miller, *Christ's thorn or the Jerusalem thorn (see fig. 4). (Design of Fiori, Paoletti & Beguinot, in* Flora Italiana illustrata*).*

as dozens of different kinds of pollen, moulds and, perhaps, bacteria hidden among the threads of the cloth.

A world of Chinese boxes

It is a world of Chinese boxes, which within the few square metres of the fabric encompasses the structures – of the dimensions of millimetres – of its weave and of particles of spice; those measurable in thousandths of a millimetre, of the fibres joined together in the threads of the weave, of pollen grains and micro-organisms; those infinitesimally tiny (millionths of a millimetre) of micro-fibrils and cellulose molecules, the raw material of the Shroud fabric . . .

A world uniting archaeology with biology, the Holy Scriptures with the history of pharmacy, the study of ancient and present-day flowers with chemistry and physics, and opening a way – little known yet fecund in results – to an understanding of the Shroud Relic.

A world revealing, among other things, how even in science God chooses the little things by which to confound the mighty, and how, from a scientific point of view, only the first step has as yet been taken along the road to understanding the Shroud.

Our most immediate step in pursuing this journey is to start with what we can see with the naked eye (the sheet as such), so as later to arrive at the infinitely little (the cellulose molecules of which it is composed). From the plant from which the cloth has been produced, to the material of which it consists, to the traces encompassing and documenting its history, the distance to be covered is too long for the space we have at our disposal. Yet we can but try and perhaps it will not be labour lost.

Flax, the plant the Shroud is made of

The Shroud fabric is a piece of linen measuring 4.36 metres long by 1.10 metres wide, which in the sixteenth century was sewn onto a piece of white cloth (holland cloth), hemmed round in the eighteenth century with a blue border weighted with metal foil. The whole today is kept wrapped in a length of red silk. In other words, the cloth on which the image of the Man of the Shroud appears is a textile woven on the loom from the fibres of a textile plant still in use today, even if being progressively replaced by cotton and man-made fibres: flax (*Linum usitatissimum L.*). The most ancient textile plant of which we have documented information and certain archaeological remains, and the history of which we can reconstruct with considerable accuracy.

Flax, the plant

Flax is a cultivated herbaceous plant, varying in height from half a metre to a metre and a half; it is biennial or perennial, but is pulled up by the roots and re-sown each year. When full-grown it is easily recognisable by the shape of its smooth-

Fig. 2 – Papyrus of an Egyptian tomb in which flax plants of huge sizes are being tended by a dignitary. The picture represents a scene in the afterlife and symbolises the fertility and bliss of the new life of the defunct by the supernatural dimensions of the textile plant. (From: Museo Egizio, Civiltà degli Egizi. Vita Quotidiana).

edged, undivided leaves, its cylindrical, glabrous stems branching high up, and by the form and colours of the flowers (consisting of three sepals edged with white and five petals for the most part of a particular shade of blue – the mauve or lilac colour so much esteemed in the eighteenth century – but also white or light yellow, depending on the variety) and by its fruits (the famous linseed of our nuns' poultices), small, oval, reddish-brown with a yellow streak and covered in mucilage.

As with all cultivated plants, particular forms have gradually evolved with the passing of the centuries due to processes of selection by the farmer, and to its being transplanted into different soils and climates from those where it originated: forms appropriately called 'cultivated varieties' with differing characteristics as regards the quality and value of the products to be obtained from them.

Even though in the present context we are primarily concerned with the textile plant, the great success flax has enjoyed for thousands of years over thousands of square kilometres (from the Iranian plateau to Europe, from Egypt to Ethiopia) does not depend only on its stalks, the source of the weaving fibres, but also on the seeds from which an oil can be extracted with uses both edible and medicinal. Even today, in Ethiopia (where the cultivation of flax is very ancient and co-eval with that of spelt, going back to

Neolithic times) the flax seeds are used for making a concentrated food used as wayfarer's bread. What is more, only recently has the use of flax seeds and flax flour as an emollient and anti-inflammatory become little more than a curiosity, having previously been an esteemed and wide-spread remedy. In our own countries now however, flax is mainly used as an important source of drying oil or of solvent for varnishes (red lead, the oldest and best-known rust-preventer is liquid because it contains linseed oil).

Spread and use of flax

Today flax has spread to every continent including Australia, where however it seems to have arrived at the same time as the Europeans. It is also cultivated in India, above all in the Punjab, and in Argentina particularly to produce oil, while industrial cultivation to obtain the textile fibres is confined to the eastern territories of Europe and is gradually being reduced.

From these few points about flax, we have learnt a little information not only about its biology but, indirectly, about that of many cultivated plants. *First*: that cultivated plants can serve multiple uses; *secondly*: that the areas where they grow and the way they are used may change from time to time (in other words that cultivated plants move and migrate with the wind, with animals and with the human beings who cultivate them);

thirdly: that different parts of the one same plant can have completely different uses.

These facts tell us nothing about where flax originated, nor when it was first domesticated, nor when it came to be used in its various possible ways by human beings. To answer these questions, biological knowledge alone is not enough.

Like all cultivated plants, flax too is derived from a wild species which exploited the proximity of human beings and their dwellings. For flax is a plant with small oily seeds which can easily be scattered by animals or people and, being a nitrate-loving plant (namely one that thrives on rubbish and rubbish-heaps), it can grow luxuriantly near any human settlement. If the settlement becomes permanent, the plants developing round it can be tended, harvested regularly and used. But when and where was flax first domesticated? This is an important question too for assessing the age and country of origin of the Shroud cloth, which is itself made of flax, i.e. of a textile fibre spread over Asia, Europe and Africa.

To answer this question, biological information is not enough, even though the specialists on the origin of cultivated plants and the greatest of them all, Nikolai Vavilov, the father of this science, have been biologists. Biological data have to be combined with archaeological discoveries, geographical information and historical documents.

Until a few years ago, the earliest documents

to attest the presence and cultivation of flax were pictures and textiles dating from Ancient Egypt. There are various pre-dynastic Egyptian textiles made of flax, also textiles preserved in the famous tomb of the architect Kha and his wife Merit now kept in the Egyptian Museum in Turin. But mainly, flax, its cultivation and the operations of harvesting and spinning are perfectly shown in tomb paintings of the Egyptian Old Kingdom (see A. M. Donadoni Roveri, 1987).

The presence of flax in the Near East

Only a dozen years ago, thanks to research conducted at Nahal Nemar in Palestine by Bar Yosef of the Israeli Museum, Jerusalem, published in 1985, where and when flax was first domesticated has now been established. The date has been obtained by analysis of plant remains coming from archaeological sites of the Neolithic period and identifiable from their pollen and the remains of stalks and leaves: an investigative technique (the so-called archaeo-botanical analysis) which we shall find also being used for the Shroud.

In short, flax is a plant which was already being cultivated 6,000 years before Christ, not only at Nahal Nemar but also in Jericho (according to a publication by D. Zohary in 1986), and hence originating in the Middle East like durum wheat, common wheat, lentils, barley and peas. More precisely, flax originated in ancient Syria, north of the agricultural area of the ancient Mediterranean and south-west of the Iranian area. It was being cultivated there five thousand years ago, more or less, and well before the period when its cultivation is documented in Ancient Egypt.

From Syria it spread to Africa and Europe. It reached Africa having crossed Sinai, and was widely cultivated along the Nile. In Europe, already in the New Stone Age it appears in Denmark. In its migrations it carried along various other plants either harvested with it or closely resembling it, which have also been put to human use. Among those resembling it, i.e. plants which in their early growth look like flax and hence do not get weeded out, we may note rocket. Among those harvested with it, i.e. those plants which grow quickly among the flax plants at harvest time, we may note rape.

To sum up, if today the fortunes of flax are in decline, this does not mean that it has not had its moments of glory, and among these we must count that period two thousand years ago in Palestine when flax fabrics were used as ritual clothing for Jewish priests and as burial garments.

But the flax plant is one thing, and the textile produced from it is quite another. From metres of the plant the time has come to drop down to millimetres of weaving thread, and thousandths of a millimetre of the cells composing it.

From the flax plant to the Shroud fabric and its chemical composition

How flax is worked

To make cloth from flax, you cannot use the whole plant or stalk. First the fibres must be separated from the plant by getting rid of the useless matter which would prevent their being spun. The technique for transforming the plant into thread has not changed substantially since the period of the Ancient Egyptian pictures. What happens is that the flax stalks are harvested at various ages by uprooting them and are then left to steep in water. Staying in water, with the action of the right sort of bacteria, destroys the soft parts of the plant and liberates a particular type of cell in the stem. Tapering, varying numbers of millimetres long, composed almost entirely of cellulose, flexible and resistant, these are known in botany as fibres.

Once isolated, the fibres have to be twisted together and spun. This, by coupling one to another, makes it possible to construct threads a few millimetres thick and indefinitely long. By using a loom, the individual threads can be interwoven by constructing a warp and woof at different angles, and thus a textile may be produced.

We shall not tarry over the lengths of cloth, weaves or spinning, for these are matters for research by non-botanical specialists (for the most part archaeologists) who are experts on ancient textiles. True it is that in certain cases the botanist is not unuseful, since not all ancient textiles have reached us in a good state of preservation. Some have remained virtually intact, like the architect Kha's famous tunic in the Egyptian Museum, Turin, a tunic of heavy weave with a coloured braid round its hem and neckline. Others, like the bandages of many New Kingdom mummies, have been reduced to charred remains by the very effect of the bitumen and caustic soda with which the corpse was treated to embalm it. Thus not a few diagnoses of textile fibres in ancient textiles are defective, making their validity suspect, though this does not prevent us from showing that the Ancient Egyptians favoured white linen fabrics, while variously decorated textiles with coloured insets were preferred in the Hellenistic period.

This however does not apply to the Shroud fabric. The Shroud is a fabric of herringbone weave, well-preserved despite traces of the Chambéry fire and the presence of small, perhaps earlier, scorch-marks, and of creases which today are increasingly spreading over the cloth. In other words, the Shroud was woven with the same techniques as those used for weaving two small Egyptian funerary fabrics of the second century after Christ (Savio, 1973). The Shroud is certainly of pure flax, as has been confirmed by Baima Rollone who has analysed threads under the optic microscope and the scanning electron microscope. They show the typical structure of flax fibres (smooth, cylindrical fibres interrupted by little constrictions).

Furthermore, materials of herringbone weave have been found during excavations, organised by Kukushiki University, 80 km from ancient Babylon in Iraq and dated by carbon-14 technique to 140 BC plus or minus 100 years (Fuji, 1976).

The chemical composition of flax

It may be interesting to consider why the flax fibres, a few thousandths of a millimetre thick, can be joined together to form the thread, and

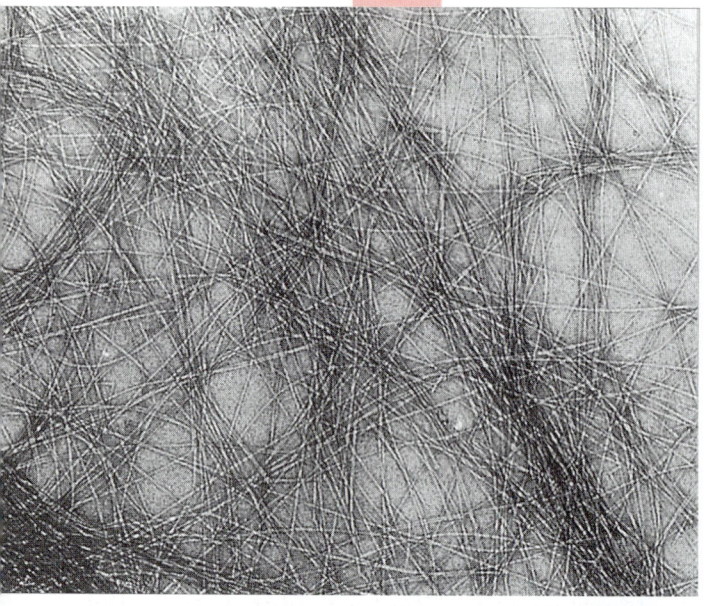

Fig. 3 – Microfibrils of cellulose isolated from the outer wall of a plant cell and enlarged about a hundred thousand times. They appear as transparent filaments of indefinite length, about 10 millionths of a millimetre thick. The steeping of the flax stalks has stripped away the amorphous mass, leaving complete microfibrils as here. From these, the thread can be obtained by spinning, to be used for weaving the cloth. (Photo: B. Vian, Paris, obtained by electron microscopy.

this in turn be transformed into a resistant cloth capable of defying the millennia. The reason lies in the chemico-physical properties of a molecule which we have constantly before our eyes, given that paper is made of cellulose and that cellulose itself is, so to speak, the principal component of the Shroud.

Cellulose is an organic compound of carbon, hydrogen and oxygen bound together in such a way as to constitute a large molecule having the form of filamentary chains. Let us support what we have been saying with a few figures. The cellulose molecules are a polymer, more precisely a poly-saccharide, in as much as they in their turn are composed of a great many little molecules, a millionth of a millimetre long and half as wide, all alike (those of a well-known sugar, glucose), joined to one another to constitute individual filamentary chains a few millimetres long. The individual chains, in their turn, join one to another in parallel, so constituting fibrils, or micro-fibrils, little more than three millionths of a millimetre thick.

It is the very structure of the cellulose microfibrils that is responsible for the textile fibre: the plant fibres' ability to be spun; the resistance of the flax thread to traction; its resistance to water. which can soak into it but not loosen it; the very ability of vegetable fabrics (not only flax but cotton and hemp too) to withstand the passage of time. For the particular bond that holds the monomers of cellulose together is resistant not only to chemical attacks but also to those of microbes. Only a very small number of microorganisms, a small number of moulds, a few bacteria and a very few protozoas are able to digest cellulose and destroy it.

Can it be dated?

Furthermore, the way the plant synthesises cellulose suggests that ancient vegetable textiles should be dateable with a technique made famous by the controversial results obtained on material from the Shroud in the United States, England and Switzerland, I mean carbon dating. This is not the place for going into either technical details or the controversy over the dating of the Shroud fabric thus obtained. A close analysis and accurate reconstruction of what happened has been published by Baima Bollone in *Sindon o no* and more recently specialists have dealt with the subject in reviews and at international congresses. Dating by radio-carbon is a delicate method; it requires complex calculations and, given the data and experiments conducted in the 1990s by the Russian physicist Kouznetsov, a specialist in the carbon-dating of ancient textiles, presented at the San Marino Congress in 1996, it also requires corrective factors to be introduced in the calculations necessary for dating, depending on the material, on its state of preservation, on the periods it has spent at high temperature (as in the case of the Shroud which suffered well-known damage from fire) and by accidental contaminants. According to his findings, the cellulose micro-fibrils of the Shroud fabric, by virtue of the chemico-physical structure, could have fixed carbon dioxide in the atmosphere during the fire in the sixteenth century, thus changing the relationship between the two isotopes of carbon on which carbon-dating is based.

To sum up, knowledge of the merely botanical aspects (from the organism to the molecule) and comparison of the data thus obtained with the archaeological documents provides a mass of information: the textile plant from which the Shroud has been made, flax, the area of origin and the ways in which the plant has spread, the type of weave, the possible time when it was woven, the uses to which similar fabrics have been put.

In the light of all this, nothing prevents the Shroud from having come from Palestine two thousand years ago.

But what is more: the linen of the Shroud has been a real "trap" for a large amount of botanical materials and remains, a mine of information and clues about the use to which the linen has been put, about the mysterious forming of the Shroud imprints, about the lands where the Shroud was woven and where it has sojourned. We shall deal with this in our next chapter.

Plants that have left traces on the Shroud

Looking for small traces

The linen of the Shroud, as such, even with all the features we have been discussing, would only be one among the many ancient fabrics that have come down to us. The Shroud linen however bears an image corresponding impressively with the Gospel account of Christ's passion. It bears traces of human blood, remains of spices, dozens of different kinds of pollen and, as we have known since 1930, a large quantity of moulds which have never yet been studied in depth.

Here we shall pass over the most important aspect of the Shroud, i.e. that it is the relic, or at least the most important icon, of Christ's passion: the imprint of the Man of the Shroud with the blood-stains and signs of his wounds and injuries. Other people more competent than I deal with this in other volumes of our series.

We shall confine ourselves to searching out the little things, the secondary aspects, the other signs left on the linen by events that accompanied and followed the forming of the image. Because exploration of the linen in quest of traces has perforce been limited to restricted parts of it (all the pollen studied so far has come from a surface area of 240 square centimetres), this does not rule out the possibility that research into vegetable and microbic traces may have surprises in store. For already, today, the information yielded by these materials is by no means negligible and gives us valuable clues to the use and history of the Shroud cloth. From botanical traces, information can be extracted about the Man of the Shroud (indirect as it may be) and also about the history of his image, and immediately a close connection is discovered between the vegetable traces on the Shroud and the plants in the Bible.

The thorn-bush and the wounds of the crown of thorns

The Shroud image itself bears an important botanical trace, that of the wounds from a cap of thorns. A crown of thorns not corresponding to classic iconography, precisely because it is not a crown but a cap. This fact and the shape of the thorns (which have left their trace) are in perfect accord with the identification of the crown-of-thorns plant proposed by Ha-Reubeni of the University of Jerusalem in 1933 (see M. Zohari, 1970).

Before going into the question, it seems worthwhile remembering that studies in botanical knowledge of ancient civilisations (far from rare when all is said and done) have made it possible to construct lists with the modern names of plants which were called something else by the ancients. Today, citing at random, we have lists of plants which were used by the ancient Chinese, Indians, Cretans, Egyptians, Greeks, Latins, Mayans. This is information of great historical usefulness, given the importance of plants in ancient cultures as food, medicine, fuel, building material.

Knowledge about plants used by ancient civilisations is particularly advanced (and has been for some time) on the plants of the Bible. To find out about these, one should refer to the *Enciclopedia della Bibbia* published by Elle Di Ci, Turin, in 1970. Here, under the heading *flora biblica*, compiled by M. Zohary, Professor of Botany at the Hebrew University, Jerusalem, some hundred species are identified, discussed and evaluated in relation to the culture and economy of the Jewish people. Not many, given that the present flora of Palestine numbers three thou-

Fig. 4 – Paliurus spina-Christi *Miller, the white-thorn and classic candidate for the crown of thorns, the same plant as* Zizyphus spina-Christi *L., which retains the name given by Linnaeus. One of many examples of the confusion in botanical terms and synonyms. (Drawing by M. Zohary in* Flora palaestina).

sand two hundred species, but not few either! Among these plants some are simply called thorns (*sirin* in Hebrew, *spinae* in the Vulgate), and among these is concealed the plant from which the Shroud's cap of thorns was taken, like the one shown in the painting in the Catacombs of Praetextatus (dated, give or take a little, AD 150).

So from the positioning of the lesions on the head of the Shroud image, from the plant's spiny branches, its wide diffusion in Palestine, its common use as kindling for lighting the fire, we can identify the cap-of-thorns plant as *Poterium spinosum* L. or *Sarcopoterium spinosum*, Schrantz, our crown of thorns (see fig. 1). A diagnosis which today is indirectly supported by the presence of its pollen on the Shroud, as demonstrated by Max Frei.

Not even Linnaeus is infallible

Examination of the image of the Man of the Shroud's head thus supports the way the crown of thorns is depicted in the Catacombs of Praetextatus as against more recent iconography. It gives the lie to the founder of systematic biology, Karl Linnaeus, who on the basis of similarity with the thorns preserved at Pisa, Trier and Notre-Dame in Paris, thought *Zizyphus spina-Christi* to be the plant from which the crown of thorns had been plucked, and named it accordingly. But this species does not survive the

Jerusalem winter and can thus be set aside as a candidate for the crown of thorns. The same goes for other species of Zizyphus either too rare in Palestine or localised far from Jerusalem. Truth to tell, among the pollen grains Frei identified on the Shroud (of which we shall have more to say later), he did also find that of *Zizyphus spina-Christi* L. which may be considered as synonymous with *Paliurus spina-Christi* Miller. But the various species of Zizyphus are hard to tell apart by pollen analysis alone, and the question then instantly arises as to whether there was once a time when *Zizyphus spina-Christi* normally completed its life-cycle in Jerusalem, or whether Frei's diagnosis resulted from over-reliance on the possibility of making such precise distinctions between pollen granules.

Thus the study of the Shroud image and present-day knowledge on the botany of Palestine (the Palestinian flora has hardly changed from then to the '70s of our own century, if we accept the view of M. Zohary, author of the monumental *Flora Palaestina*) have perhaps contradicted the authority of the greatest botanist of all time, but indirectly make us wonder what degree of precision the diagnoses of the greatest expert in the palynology of the Shroud could attain.

It goes without saying that establishing which the plant of the crown of thorns was is not something all that essential as regards the account of Christ's passion, and smacks of a rather petty pedantry even to discuss it. Yet even little things can help us to reflect, be it to grasp how the simplest of problems can in fact be complex when we are dealing with archaeological materials (to which the Shroud most certainly belongs), or to recognise that no analytical techniques exist that are absolutely fool-proof.

It is in any case indisputable that among the 'little things', those very traces of vegetable matter and its derivatives have a significance far from negligible for a scientific understanding of the Shroud image.

How the Shroud image was formed is still, in fact, a matter for controversy. However, a significant contribution to the forming of the imprint might well come from the mass of photo-sensitive spices sprinkled over the body of the Man of the Shroud and the exudations from the dying body or from the corpse.

The viability of this hypothesis depends on one fact: whether, that is, there are traces of oil or spices on the linen. The presence of traces of aloes and myrrh on the Shroud has been regarded as a matter of fact since research first began but it has only been confirmed for certain since Baima Bollone used specific ultra-sensitive anti-serums on threads which he had himself removed from the Shroud.

Yet to find out exactly what aloes and myrrh are is not a waste of effort. We shall talk about them at length, since by doing so we shall come to realise how the diagnoses of products of past ages refer us to real Chinese boxes of problems within problems, and how botany, chemistry, archaeology and forensic medicine, as well as reaching unconflicting conclusions, end up collaborating to the point of virtually swapping jobs.

Traces of aloes

Aloe, or more exactly the various species of aloe, the classification of which is complicated and controversial, are plants of a dry environment, succulent, spiny with showy flowers. Today spread all over the world, they are a species related to the lilies, the asphodels and, more directly, to the big agaves now acclimatised and wide-spread even along the Ligurian Riviera. The species from which aloe was extracted in antiquity were, as far as we can tell from historical documents, *Aloe vera* Auct. not L. (Pignatti, 1982) and *Aloe socotrina* Lam., both plants of African origin. Today *Aloe vera* grows wild along the coasts of the Mediterranean, and in Italy is particularly abundant on the coasts of Calabria and Sicily. It probably arrived on the coasts of Europe in classical antiquity in the wake of the Phoenicians. In the territories of the Roman Empire it was a notable success and maintained its place among medicinal plants from the days of classical Greece through medieval times right up to the present day. Its territories of origin and its presence in

Phoenician hands make it likely it was also to be found on the coasts of Palestine and the Lebanon. Aloes are documented as wild plants throughout the Middle East and in Ancient Egypt, and their use is amply documented in Egypt and the ancient Middle East (see Gerola, 1962). So the aloe of the official Italian pharmacopia, the dry condensed juice of the plant

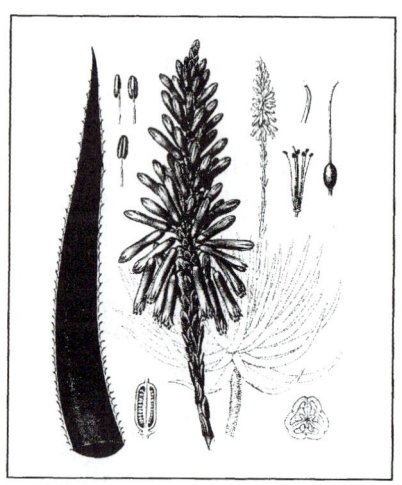

Fig. 5

Figs. 5 and 6 – An example of the interpretative problems concerning plants used in antiquity and their corresponding to modern classifications. Two completely different plants are 'identified' as the Aloe: Aloe socotrina Lam., one of the aloes from which the aloes of the Italian pharmacopia is extracted. This is a bitter, resinous extract from a succulent plant, as opposed to Aquilaria agallocha Roxb., the tree from which a bitter powder is extracted, aloes-wood or the aloes of the Ayurvedic pharmacopia of India. (From: KOEHLERS, Medizinal-Pflanzen in naturgetreven Abbildungen, Gera-Vutehaums, 1887-1898, 3 vols, and from Kirtikar and others, 1935.

which comes in brown or blackish coloured lumps or irregular fragments with a distinctive scent and very bitter taste, should more or less be that of the ancient Mediterranean, the Near East, Palestine and the Shroud. For the aloes of the Bible and ancient Egyptian documents is not the plant as such but a bitter product extracted mainly from its leaves or perhaps a powder got by grinding the plant. We should not however rule out the possibility that the Biblical aloe may contain a bitter powder obtained from the wood of *Aquilaria agallocha* Roxb. *Aquilaria agallocha* is a large evergreen tree of the family of the Thymelaeaceae which grows in the Himalayan range and in Assam, whence it has come from

Fig. 6

the Far East. The wood is oily and fragrant; in powder form it is used as a perfume for the skin and for clothes; a scented resin is extracted from it. In English it is known as aloe-wood, in as much as it is bitter and fragrant but has a disagreeable taste. It is much used in Yunnanese and Ayurvedic medicine as a stimulant and astringent (see Kirtikar and others, 1935). It would be to discuss whether this wood could have anything to do with the aloes and the perfumes compounded of aloes cited by Zohary? *Aloe vera* Auct. not L. (Pignatti, 1982) and *Aloe socotrina* Lam. (Liliaceae) are also known to Yunnanese and Ayurvedic medicine for treating bilious attacks and getting rid of intestinal worms (Ayurveda).

The same goes for the *Commiphora* (synonymous with *Balsamodendron*) among which we even find a *Commiphora myrrha* Engl.

This is another example of interpretational problems with 'ancient' plants, if we only have historical documents at our disposal. Problems of this sort can be resolved today thanks to availability of very refined analytical techniques, as for instance those of immunology, making it possible to recognise matter even if much altered morphologically. This demonstrates how helpful a biological archive of archaeological materials can be in interpreting archaeological documents.

To sum up, the aloes whose medical fortunes have recently made a come-back owing to their being used in cosmetics and because it seems they contain potentially anti-carcinogenic compounds, are medicinal plants with a history lost in the mists of time. Among biblical plants, the aloe often recurs as a perfume, or as an aromatic, and even as a condiment for food. This last use, certainly unattested among our own dietary habits, is not as strange as it may seem at first sight, given that in our own day in Japan the aloe is one of the ingredients in a soup, highly esteemed and wide-spread, called *mizu*.

It is interesting to note how in the Bible aloes and myrrh are associated as high-quality perfumes ('... myrrh and aloes with all the best spices' we read in the Song of Songs), and that various 'incenses' or mixtures to produce perfumed smoke contain aloes. Lastly we should remember that aloes and myrrh were used for the burial of Jesus. According to the Gospel of John (19:39), Nicodemus brought about 100 pounds weight of myrrh and aloes (30 kg. more or less) for Christ's burial.

Traces of myrrh

Myrrh is the resinous secretion of various species of the genus *Commiphora*, small trees with spiny branches bearing red flowers, belonging to the family of the Burseraceae, a family of tropical plants characterised by the presence in the live tissues of secretory canals containing resins and

Fig. 7 – One of a number of myrrh-producing trees: Balsamodendron myrrha *Nees v. Es. In the Italian pharmacopia, myrrh (Myrrhae tinctura or tincture of myrrh) is an extract from the gum-resin secreted by the trunk and branches of* Commiphora molmol *Engl. Many other* Commiphoras, *plants closely related to the Balsamodendrons which some authors consider a particular species of Commiphora, can produce myrrh and among them our own particular choice for the myrrh of antiquity,* Commiphora abyssinica *Engl. (From* KOEHLERS, Medizinal – Pflanzen in naturgetreven Abbildungen, Gera-Vutehaums, *1887-1898, 3 vols. and from* Kirtikar and others, *1935.)*

aromatic oleoresins (see Gerola, 1962). About a dozen species of the genus Commiphora produce myrrh, that is, oily aromatic compounds of various colours but for the most part yellowish, which ooze spontaneously from the bark of the plant or can be extracted by incisions in the right places. These oleoresins, which go dark-brown when dry, are myrrh, a name derived from the Aramaic *mura* (= bitter) which perfectly describes the salient characteristic of the product. Myrrh, as we know it today, comes in the form of granules or small irregular lumps, reddish or reddish-brown, with a bitter taste and a fresh and pleasing smell.

The main myrrh-producing species is *Commiphora abyssinica* Engl., which, as its name indicates, is native to northern Abyssinia, but other very similar species growing in Somalia, Arabia and India produce myrrh too.

Used in past centuries as an anti-diarrhoeal and to alleviate gastric pains, today myrrh, a recognised item in the Italian pharmacopia, is still used occasionally but only for external use for its astringent and antiseptic properties.

The history of myrrh however, like that of aloes, is lost in the mists of time, with the result that it is often mentioned in the Bible where its most widely documented use is as perfume. Suffice it to remember the Song of Songs with its list of perfumes: '*What is this coming up from the desert like a column of smoke, breathing of myrrh and frankincense and every exotic perfume?* (3:6) ... *myrrh and aloes with all the best spices...*' (4:14). Myrrh with aloes went into the composition of the perfume *qetoreth*, the *incensum* of the Vulgate, in which, in the days of the historian Josephus

Flavius (in the first century AD) a good thirteen different ingredients were mixed. The *qetoreth* was offered on a special altar and profane use of it was forbidden, but this did not prevent myrrh with its charms from being in common use as personal perfume for women, as it is written in the already quoted Song of Songs: '*like a sachet of myrrh, he lies between my breasts*' (1:13).

Various uses of myrrh

The use of myrrh as a perfume was not confined to the Jews. The Great Kings of Persia perfumed their dwellings with myrrh. Among the ancient Egyptians, myrrh was used at feasts and sacred ceremonies as is shown, among other things, by the hymn to Hathor, goddess of dancing and pleasure: '*For you are the lady of the round-dance, the queen of Plaited garlands. the lady of myrrh, the queen of the dance…*' The prizing of myrrh in the Near East dates from the earliest of historic times and led to the development of proper trade-routes from Arabia to Palestine and Syria, and from Somalia and Nubia to Egypt. It mustn't be forgotten that the gifts brought to the Infant Jesus by the Magi (priests and sages from the East whom some people think to have been sage-disciples of Zoroaster) include myrrh.

Myrrh also had medicinal uses linked with its sleep-inducing and antiseptic properties, which are still recognised today.

The Gospel of Mark (15:23) mentions the use of *vinum myrrhatum*, i.e. myrrh dissolved in wine as a sedative and anaesthetic for those condemned to crucifixion. *Vinum myrrhatum* was offered to Jesus for him to drink before being crucified. Myrrh and other aromatics dissolved in olive oil composed the oil for anointing Jewish priests. The use of myrrh in embalming rites is documented in Ancient Egypt (where, only in the case of hasty or low-cost preparation techniques, were vegetable spices replaced with bitumen) and also, as we have seen, in Jewish burial rites of the time of Jesus.

The vaporographic theory

Thus the presence on the linen of aloes, myrrh and blood, the Gospel account of the anointing of the Crucified, the possibility that evaporation from the spices, sweat and blood-serum might 'impress' stable imprints on the linen, could not but become the basis for a 'vaporographic' theory about the forming of the image. Put briefly: the stains from aloes, myrrh and blood would be a kind of 'misprint' due to excess of matter, while the Shroud image would be made from more or less the same matter as the stains. This hypothesis enjoyed great success at the beginning of this century. It has been modified to some degree by various authors since. In one exceptional case, the entire Shroud image has been attributed to transference of the spices on to the cloth. Such is the hypothesis of Giovanni Donna d'Aldenico (an expert on the history of agriculture and local history, who was president of the Turin Academy of Agriculture as well as founder and president of the Lanzo Valleys History Society). At the beginning of the 1970s and referring back to the observations made on herbarium pages by the French pharmacist Volckringer, he proposed that the Shroud imprint was due to the transference of phenols (a blackish component present in vegetable cells in abundance) onto the linen. The Shroud image would thus be the effect of a true printing process of the body underneath, fixed in time by the great stability of phenolic compounds. It is hard to find a hypothesis more 'botanical' than this: the Shroud image would have been formed by exactly the same mechanism as that whereby a drying plant leaves its imprint on blotting-paper (it too composed of cellulose like the Shroud fabric). It is an intelligent hypothesis too, but – alas – like all vaporographic theories, does not solve the problem.

Other hypotheses

Today, thanks to the painstaking research of an American-led international group (The Shroud of Turin Group), we know that the Shroud image was formed by a rapid dehydration and oxidisation of the cellulose fibres of the sheet; but we know, thanks to Baima Bollone's research, that even the threads in the zone of the Shroud image can support the same kind of matter as that of the various stains. That the Shroud image was formed by some kind of accelerated ageing of the cellulose fibres does not however rule out the possibility that substances, no longer there today, may have been responsible or jointly responsible for the phenomenon. But this is another topic, to be discussed elsewhere.

So the traces of the spices have not resolved the problem of 'how' the image was formed, but are fully compatible with the account of Christ's passion handed down to us by St John and with our own knowledge, both botanical and archaeological, about Palestine in the days of Jesus. In other words, the stains of spices, the traces of the thorn-wounds, our own archaeological and archaeo-botanical knowledge, strengthen the hypothesis that the Shroud is the winding-sheet of a man who was tortured with a cap of thorns and then put to death by crucifixion.

The Shroud linen however hides other types of information and other problems to be solved, in very particular micro-traces: pollen grains which it has trapped over its long history.

Pollen grains have nothing to do with the formation of the Shroud image but have much to say about the Shroud's history: this will be well worth our careful attention.

Pollen and the history of the Shroud

Scholars turn their attention to pollen

With pollen – tiny granules with forms, dimensions and structures superficially differing from plant to plant – our attention turns to objects of microscopic dimensions, a few thousandths of a millimetre. Pollen forms part of the abundant extraneous matter which has gradually accumulated on the Shroud cloth, and which has been captured by applying sticky tape to the fabric, or by being vacuumed up from the cloth and from the space between the linen of the Shroud and its Holland backing. The pollen has been analysed mainly by the Swiss botanist and criminologist Frei, and to a lesser extent by the Turinese forensic expert and sindonologist Baima Bollone, and by the U.S. study group on the Shroud.

It is material which in recent years has been attracting more and more attention and is certainly worth talking about here. But let us do everything in order and begin with what pollen grains are and what they are made of.

What pollen is and what it is made of

Pollen granules are produced inside the anthers (micro-capsules) a few millimetres in size, which develop on the variously coloured filaments surrounding the ovaries in the flowers of plants. Pollen grains are also produced by plants such as pines and firs which do not form true flowers. In these cases the pollen is borne by specialised scales which enclose it in a kind of case. Ferns and mosses on the other hand do not have pollen at all, but produce reproductive structures similar in form to pollen but biologically very different: spores. Even with their tiny dimensions, a few thousandths of a millimetre in diameter, pollen grains have complicated forms and an essential function for the life of plants, in that they contain the male elements guaranteeing plants' sexual reproduction.

To grasp how important pollen is in scientific research on the Shroud (and more generally in forensic medicine and modern archaeology, so much so as to figure in a research programme co-ordinated by the Italian National Research Council for the evaluation of cultural assets), it is necessary to have precise knowledge of its morphological and functional characteristics.

In brief terms, a grain of pollen is a single cell with more nuclei, protected by a thick outer wall impermeable to water and to gases in the atmosphere, a kind of survival capsule, of differing forms (spherical, sub-spherical, ellipsoid, variously lobate), more or less constant in the same plant but differing more or less from plant to plant. All the biological properties which the granule enjoys depend in the final analysis however not on its form but on the structure and chemical composition of its cellular outer wall.

The structure of pollen

The cellular outer wall of the pollen granule is a microscopic, multi-layered structure. Moving from the outside inwards, we first of all find a layer more or less thick (a few thousandths of a millimetre, called the extine) and a thinner layer made up of pectins and cellulose which is generally called the intine. For our purposes, the more significant and interesting part is the extine. The extine is made up of extremely resistant carbon compounds, consisting of chains of hydrocarbons linked together in all directions. It is impermeable to water and gases, and resists digestion by the most varied chemical compounds, and compression without becoming distorted. As the extine resists attack by chemical and physical means, so also it resists attack by animals, insects and micro-organisms.

The extine hardly ever forms a perfectly smooth layer and if the surface is examined under the microscope interesting details may be discovered. In some zones it may present dents, it may present small perforations, may grow thinner or thicker. The interesting fact is that the shape and dimensions of these modifications of the extine (which are truly ornamental) are different in different species of plants.

The picture of a pollen grain magnified 500 times by the scanning electron microscope, which lets us have a three-dimensional image of it, revealing details indistinguishable by other means, is clearer than any description in words (see cover illustration, and its caption on page 1).

At this point it is virtually inevitable for us to realise that the form, dimensions and ornamentations of the pollen grain make it possible to attribute it to the plant that originally produced it, and that whatever pollen is captured by whatever support (a handful of soil, a lichen, a moss, an adhesive strip, a piece of cloth, a filter) can be recognised and identified by any skilled botanist armed with a decent microscope. Further, since the grains are extremely resistant and remain virtually unaltered for thousands of years, they can also be found in remarkable quantities in various geological strata and in different archaeological materials. Naturally, after thousands and thousands of years the pollen grains are dead. All the same, they are always recognisable. This makes it possible to extract information very accurately reconstructing the pollen population present in a given terrain (and at a given period, if there is information available for dating it, such as archaeological specimens, historical documents, palaeontological data). From the ensemble of facts about pollen, which is called the 'pollen spectrum', one may go back to the plants that produced the various types, i.e. to the flora and vegetation of the place where and time when the pollen was produced.

Types of pollen on the Shroud

This being so, it follows that palynology has become a very important auxiliary tool for archaeology. Through types of pollen found one can go back to the landscape, agriculture, content of the vegetable components of food, market produce, perfumes, products for pharmaceutical use, of former times. Not for nothing are numerous research programmes in train today (in Italy and elsewhere) to collect 'archives' of biological traces, among which pollen plays a prominent role, as aid to anthropological and archaeological research.

This explains why the Swiss botanist and criminologist Frei in the 1970s suggested research into the pollen on the Shroud, with the support of the Turin Centre of Sindonology. This made it possible for him not only to analyse the grains of pollen removed from the Shroud, but also to compare them with pollen archives of Palestinian, and more generally, Near Eastern plants. A direct contribution to the study of Shroud pollen has also been made by the Turinese forensic scientist and sindonologist Baima Bollone, already mentioned several times in this booklet.

But, as in life, so even more in analytical techniques and scientific theories, nothing is perfect.

Identifying the pollen

In theory, all types of pollen of whatever species of plant can be recognised and identified; in practice, some species are easy to differentiate, others are virtually indistinguishable one from another. We can with absolute certainty distinguish a walnut pollen grain from that of a beech. We should be hard put to it to tell the difference between wheat and oat. In many cases it does not matter much if instead of identifying the exact species we can identify the genus to which the species belongs, but sometimes very similar species live in very different environments and can give entirely contradictory signals. For example, many *Artemesiae*, aromatic plants among which is the famous wormwood of the Italian Alps, have very similar pollen, but we should get a very different signal, depending on whether we were to diagnose *Artemesia verlotorum* (a ruin-loving plant common in Italy) or *Artemesia herba-alba* (widespread in Syria and Anatolia). To this we must add that any plant, besides producing perfectly normal pollen, also produces malformed pollen. Hence, to be on the safe side, diagnosis should be made on the strength of a large number of granules of the same provenance, and it is not always easy to have these, given that different species produce greater or lesser amounts of pollen. For instance, those plants whose pollen is transported by insects (the *Entomophilae*) produce much less pollen than do those plants whose pollen is wind-borne (the *Anemophilae*). So it is obvious that one is more likely to find a wind-borne pollen on a given piece of material than an insect-borne specimen: and this by the simple calculation of the probabilities of different types of pollen grain being captured on an inert support.

It is equally obvious that information about pollen will be quite useless for dating the material from which it is taken, unless the flora has completely changed with the passing of time (in other words, unless we are working on extremely ancient materials, or as is now fashionable to say 'in palaeo-palynology') or if by other means we know the times of more recent minor changes (in other words, we are working on materials of historic or immediately prehistoric times, or as is now the mode to say 'in archaeo-palynology, which we can document some other way).

This is not the case with the Shroud pollen, since the data at our disposal about the flora of Palestine, Anatolia and Savoy in historic times has been substantially stable.

At any rate, those 240 sq.cm. which we mentioned earlier on, allowed Frei to recover and identify some dozens of different species of pollen, and these have provided very interesting clues to the Shroud's history, being substantially in agreement with popular and religious tradition as regards the Shroud's journey from Palestine to Savoy,

Clues or proofs?

They are *clues* and not *proofs*. Or, to put it better, they are pieces of circumstantial evidence, since the number of grains with which Frei had to work was very small. Some species of plants which he identified belong to *genera* the different species of which are hard to distinguish on the basis of pollen. Nor can it be established, at least with present-day knowledge, which pollen was deposited first and which later, though clues are not negligible.

Indeed three fundamental results have been obtained by palynology:

– a remarkable number of the pollen grains identified belong to species found in Palestine, the Arab lands or Anatolia (for instance: Aleppo pine, pistachio, Nile tamarisk, cedar of Lebanon, castor-oil plant);

– some of the pollen belongs to Central European vegetation and perfectly corresponds to that of Alpine mountainous regions (for instance: alder, beech, hazelnut, hornbeam, plane) or plants cultivated there, such as rye, indirectly confirming the worth of the palynological method in as much as they are in perfect accord with the Shroud's stay – documented beyond shadow of doubt from historical data – amid plants populating the area of Central Europe and, specifically Savoy and Piedmont;

– as regards the plants of Palestine and Anatolia, the most amply represented are those whose pollen is transported by insects; plants which are very wide-spread but whose pollen is wind-borne are lacking, and there are no traces of wheat or olive.

The data thus gathered tend to rule out discovery of major contamination (theoretically possible) by pollen carried great distances by the wind and coming from regions where the Shroud material has never made a stop.

Indeed, the types of pollen of the Anatolian and Syro-Palestinian regions (i.e. those regions on which the shafts of criticism have been most sharply concentrated), by virtue of their belonging, in part, to species pollinated by insects which produce only small amounts of pollen, can hardly be ascribed to contamination due to air-currents.

Frei's results therefore confirm that the Shroud has really spent time in Palestine, Anatolia and, as documented beyond shadow of doubt, in recent times and today in Savoy and in Piedmont.

Strictly speaking, nothing can tell us in which direction the journey took place, but we know the Shroud appeared in Europe in the late Middle Ages and since then has never left. One is therefore forced to admit the Shroud originally came from Palestine and Anatolia.

Obviously these data presuppose the absolute accuracy of all the diagnoses made by Frei and they have nothing to tell us about the era for which the Shroud's sojourn is confirmed. It would therefore be of decisive importance to have access to a larger area of the Shroud than that from which the specimens of pollen have so far been taken, so that we can increase our knowledge of its pollen spectrums.

Clues to be followed up

And here a problem arises about method, which was also discussed at length at the International Sindonological Congress at San Marino in 1996 (S. Scannerini, 1996).

As already mentioned above, the pollen of the same plant species, while corresponding to a general, common organisational plan, can present aberrations which distance it from the original model. One therefore needs a minimum number of pollen grains (about a hundred, by the present conventions in force) of the same provenance before one can make a reliable attribution of species. The risk from which it is thus intended to protect us is that of using a single pollen grain or small aberrant group as one's point of reference, which can then lead to a mistaken diagnosis. Not only this: to be able to make a diagnosis of species, it is essential to have secure standards of reference (for instance, pollen taken from herbarium samples of properly classified attribution) and make an diagnosis by comparison. This constraint is reinforced by the fact that the actual identification of the plant is important, but more important still is to discover, as we have seen earlier, what exactly was meant in time past by names still in use in our language today, or by names belonging to obsolete systems of classification. But there is more: one indisputable fact, which we have touched on a little while ago, hangs like a sword of Damocles over diagnoses which are too precise: in some *genera* (i.e. the totality of closely related individual species), distinguishing the pollen of the different species is easy, but in many it is practically impossible by present means. Lastly, the technique for preparing the pollen for examination under the microscope is not devoid of risks. These range from contamination by extraneous pollen during preparation of the slides, to artificial modification (artifact) during preparation by use of imperfect or inadequate viewing techniques. In addition to these difficulties, we cannot avoid having to observe the pollen 'just as things are', which may not yield sufficiently detailed pictures. Worse, the sample may not be in a state to endure observation by scanning microscopy. Perhaps the situation will improve with the use of new types of scanning electron microscopes, acting less destructively on the pollen grains, and more suitable for showing minute and perishable details; but a *priori* who can tell?

In other words, to confirm Frei's findings, we should need to know all about the techniques he used, know exactly how many pollen grains he analysed, know precisely what standards he referred to for his diagnoses. In short, the simplest way would be to have the original slides made available which he himself prepared, and his laboratory records. Unfortunately Frei's collection of slides was sold off by his heirs and cannot be had for reanalysis. Very little photographic material was published and the records of Frei's experiments are only fleetingly touched on in his writings.

In other words, only by disposing of data, which today we have not got, could we obtain significant answers to the three questions immediately springing to mind:

– To what species of plants as yet undiagnosed

do the grains of pollen eluding research up to now, hidden in the Shroud cloth, belong?

– Is the 'new' pollen and, above all, the pollen of species already diagnosed, still trapped in the cloth, of sufficient quantity for a methodically irreproachable analysis to be conducted and for a reliable 'pollen spectrum' to be extracted?

– Now that our knowledge about the plants of Palestine is much improved thanks to research into biblical flora conducted over a great many years at the Hebrew University, Jerusalem, what information on the history of the Shroud can be extracted by comparing the archaeological findings about Palestine and the Shroud's 'pollen spectrum'?

Has the Shroud any botanical surprises in store?

Moulds, i.e. microscopic fungi

We have just been seeing how botany has furnished data for understanding the image and travels of the Shroud. What we have not yet said is that botany, understood in the classic sense as the study of plants and micro-organisms, has still to be consulted over a whole range of as yet unexplored topics.

Until now no one has studied, except in general terms, the microbic populations of the Shroud, meaning by 'microbes' bacteria and moulds.

That large amounts of matter covering the cellulose fibres exists on the Shroud is documented beyond all doubt by every one of the few removals of Shroud threads that has occurred, as also by a checking of the dust.

The component of the moulds has been tritely diagnosed as filamentary fungi (*Hyphomycetes*), organisms made up of thin threads (*hyphae*) often a few thousandths of a millimetre thick, forming inextricable networks (*mycelia*). But 'the moulds' include organisms extremely different one from another. Some are able to destroy cellulose and hence potentially to damage or destroy the Shroud cloth. Many, not to say nearly all, absorb enormous quantities of carbon dioxide from the air and introduce it into their organism, since they are unable to effect photosynthesis (no fungus is able to do this), i.e. to use water, carbon dioxide and light to manufacture organic substances for themselves. So too the moulds can falsify dating, as for instance radiocarbon dating which establishes an object's age based on the moment when carbon dioxide was incorporated into the living organism. Obviously the mass of mould accumulating on the cloth and penetrating into it has to form a significant part of the fabric's total weight. Indeed the moulds go on surviving on the Shroud even today but how, and with what side-effects for the conservation of the sheet, no one knows. To find out, we should need to establish which moulds are involved, but to do this we should have to take samples of cloth, grow the moulds, study them and identify them.

Even if at first acquaintance the world of moulds may seem a negligible curiosity, today we know that moulds, or more generally fungi (for from some moulds even the large fungi develop which we come across out in the fields and woods) are a world of at least eighty thousand

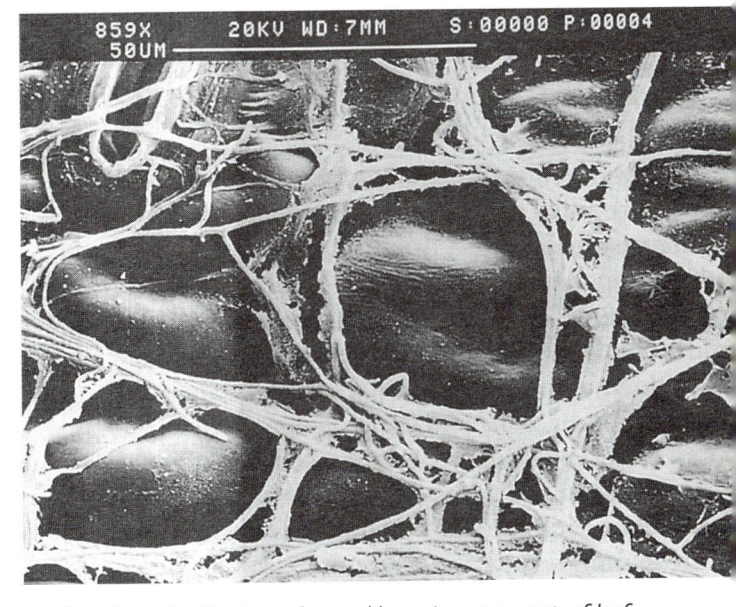

Fig. 8 – Network of hyphae of a mould growing on a scrap of leaf, seen under the scanning electron microscope. Individual hyphae are about five-thousandths of a millimetre thick; under the mat of mould may be seen the leaf-cells. (Photo by S. Scannerini, obtained by scanning electron microscopy at the Institute of Anatomy, Pharmacology and Forensic Medicine, University of Turin.)

different species which colonise the most diverse environments on our planet, including manufactured articles, fabrics, wood and toxic solutions. True, they cannot provide us with information about the Shroud's history, but they can let us glimpse the risks the Shroud will run if poorly conserved.

Bacterial populations

The same goes for the probable bacterial populations of the cloth. Bacteria are extremely small organisms (of one or less ten thousandths of a millimetre). Many are agents of disease in human beings, animals and plants. Others live in the soil or in water by breaking down the most diverse substances. Few bacteria can destroy cellulose, but many are capable of producing organic compounds by breaking down the most diverse substances.

For example, a pretty common bacterium (which lives by breaking down alcohol and producing vinegar, *Acetobacter xylinum*), instead of breaking down cellulose, manufactures it in large quantities. Other bacteria are able to manufacture viscose matter which forms a kind of mucilaginous sheath containing carbon, hydrogen and oxygen and which can coat the cellulose fibres in veritable sleeves.

In the first half of the 1990s (and the news got into the big daily newspapers), bacteria with these characteristics were isolated from Mayan fabrics in Central America. Why might they not also be present on the Shroud? Here too a completely new field of research could open up, which, even more effectively than the study of moulds, might either re-open the carbon-dating debate, or give us new perspectives on how to protect the Shroud from further degeneration. For if the moulds are nearly all dependent on the presence of gaseous oxygen and die (or at least cease to reproduce) in its absence, many bacteria survive perfectly in the absence of oxygen and are even poisoned by its presence. Of these last, some (green bacteria, purple bacteria) live by consuming water, carbon dioxide and light, i.e. by effecting photosynthesis. How many of these bacteria can produce substances damaging to the cloth, how many could little by little destroy it?

A modest suggestion for the future

There was a time when to carry out all these types of research would have involved long, very delicate work, isolation, growing the bacteria, microscopic and physiological diagnosis of all the microbes happening to be present. Today however, even minimal traces of biological matter (millionths of a gram) allow us to recognise and diagnose the organism from which it comes. There are widely applied techniques in forensic medicine, borrowed from a science developed over the last ten or so years: molecular biology. The methods of molecular biology are too technical for me to speak of in a brief chapter dealing with prospects rather than results, but these methods are commonplace enough, even though costly, to be employed on a large scale and give reliable answers.

It is enough to bear in mind that through molecular biology so far we have been able to recognise an individual bacterial organism present in a gram of dust or of soil or, if you wish, even on a flax thread or in the dust collected between the linen of the Shroud and its Holland backing.

As is always understood in scientific research, to open a new line of investigation can lead to a dead end, but it can also give completely new information of unforeseen significance. For the microbiologist, the Shroud is an environmental 'niche' maintaining a quantity of micro-traces and a microbic population which have never been studied. What surprises may a rigorous knowledge of the pollen it has captured and of the microbes living in it today have in store for us?

Perhaps new clues as to its journeyings and date, almost certainly new ideas as to how to protect it and hand it on in one piece to the generations to come.

These results are not negligible, provided we remember the significance of the Shroud lies not in the scientific object but in what it represents and commemorates for all of us.